5 STEP ENGLISH
Sleeping Beauty

5단계로 술술 읽히는 영어원서
단계 영어 잠자는 공주

초   판 | 1쇄 발행 2025년 9월 19일

지 은 이 | 빌헬름 그림, 야코프 그림
영어번역 | 스티브 오
그   림 | 김민영
정보맵핑 | 이야기 연구소
디 자 인 | 아름다운디자인
감   수 | HannahAllyse Kim
제 작 처 | 다온피앤피
특허등록 | 10-2717987
국제출원 | PCT/KE202/002551

펴 낸 곳 | (주)도서출판동행
펴 낸 이 | 오승근
출판등록 | 2020년 3월 20일 제2020-000005호
주   소 | 부산광역시 부산진구 동천로 109, 9층
이 메 일 | withyou@withyoubooks.com
카카오톡 | @동행출판사

단계별 요약정보 기술은 국내특허등록 및 PCT 국제출원을 했습니다.

이 책은 저작권법에 따라 보호받는 저작물이므로 무단 전재와 복제를 금지하며,
이 책 내용의 전부 또는 일부를 이용하려면 반드시 출판사의 서면 동의를 받아야 합니다.
잘못된 책은 구입하신 서점에서 바꿔 드립니다.

ISBN 979-11-91648-49-2(13740)

Audio Book

5단계로 술술 읽히는 영어원서

단계영어

잠자는 공주

머리말
Prologue

영어 실력이 자랄수록
영어책도 진화해야 합니다.

　자녀 신발이나 옷 사주실 때 한 치수 큰 거 사주시죠? 금방 자라니까요. 아이의 머릿속 사고도 금방 자랍니다. 사고가 자랄수록 영어책도 자라야 합니다.

　어린 나뭇가지를 방치하면 제멋대로 구부러지고 휘어 자랍니다. 반대로 어릴 때 누워있는 가지를 세워서 곧은 부목을 대고 실을 감아 놓으면 그대로 반듯하게 자랍니다. 아이도 똑같죠. 매번 나무를 뽑아 버리고 더 큰 나무를 새로 심지 마세요. 하나의 나무를 키워나가게 가르치세요. 이 책은 하나의 스토리를 수준에 맞게 5단계로 발전시켜 나가는 신개념 영어 도서입니다!

　한 번 아이들이 말을 배우는 과정을 생각해 보세요. '엄마', '아빠'와 같이 몇 안 되는 단어만 말하던 아이가 시간이 지나면 말이 길어지고 내용이 깊어집니다. 그러니까 처음엔 였는데, 시간이 지나면 처럼 표현에 깊이가 생긴다는 것입니다. 하지만 여기서 중요한 사실은, 표현은 달라졌지만 말하고자 하는 핵심 내용은 같다는 것입니다. (또는 배고프다)입니다.

　단계별 영어 동화 구성은 마치 아이들이 3~4년에 걸쳐서 언어가 성장하는 과정을 레벨 1~5에 넣은 것과 같습니다. 레벨1이 4살 아이의 표현이라면, 레벨2는 5살 아이의 표현이라 볼 수 있습니다. 전달하고자 하는 핵심 내용은 원문과 같지만, 그것을 표현하는 방식이 레벨에 따라 달라집니다.

　계단을 오르듯이 레벨별로 한 번 읽어보시기를 바랍니다.

Steve Oh

As your English skills grow,
English books should evolve accordingly.

When you buy shoes or clothes for your child, you probably buy them one size larger? Because they are growing up. Thought in the mind of a child grows quickly, too. As the thought grows, English books should grow together.

If young twigs are left unattended, they will grow bent and crooked. On the other hand, if you support a branch which lies on the earth by putting a straight splint on it, and winding a thread, it will grow straight as it is. The child is the same. Do not pluck a tree every time and plant a new tree, which is larger. Teach them to grow a tree. This book is a new concept English book that develops a story in 5 stages according to the level of the reader!

Think of the process of children learning to speak. A child who used to say only a few words such as and can utter longer words and their speech comes to have deeper meaning as time passes. So, at first they say , but as time goes on, the expression becomes more complicated, like . But the important point here is that the intention of the speech is the same, although the words are different. The fact is .

The composition of I Can Read English is as if we put the course of language development of children over 3 to 4 years into the level of 1 to 5. If Level 1 is the expression of a 4-year-old child, Level 2 is the expression of a 5-year-old child. The core content they want to convey is the same, but the way they express differs depending on the level.

I hope you read it once for each level as if you were climbing the stairs.

Steve Oh

사용설명서
Manual

단계별 영어 도서
오디오북 채널

영어는 언어입니다. 언어는 암기보단, 실제 사용을 통해 익혀야 합니다. 즉, 의미가 있어야 하고 내가 사용해야 합니다. 이 책은 학습지가 아닌 책으로서 영어를 의미 있게 사용할 수 있게 제작했습니다.

간단 하지만 명확하게 도서 사용 방법을 말씀드리겠습니다.

1. 영어 공부가 아닌 책을 읽는다고 생각하세요.

2. **레벨 1부터 읽으세요.** 레벨 1이 무척 쉽게 보여도 일단 레벨 1부터 읽어야 다음 단계로 수월하게 올라갈 수 있습니다. 마치 계단을 오를 때, 첫 계단에 발을 내디디고 그다음 계단으로 오르는 것처럼 말입니다.

3. **모르는 단어가 보이면 사전을 찾지 마세요.** 다시 한번 말씀드리지만, 이 건 책입니다. 책은 읽어야 합니다. 우리가 보통 책을 읽을 때 국어사전을 찾으면서 읽지 않는 것처럼 말입니다.

4. **레벨 5까지 읽었다면 이제 레벨 4, 3 순으로 거꾸로 읽어 보세요.** 복잡한 문장들이 어떻게 간략하게 요약되는지를 배울 수 있게 됩니다.

사용법은 위 4가지면 충분합니다.
자, 그럼 이제 시작해 볼까요?

※ 레벨5에서는 사전을 찾으셔도 됩니다. 내용 이해를 위해서가 아닌, 모르는 단어의 정확한 의미 파악을 위해 사전을 찾으셔도 됩니다.

Audio Book Channel

English is a language. Language should be learned through practical use rather than memorization. That means, it has to make sense and you have to use it. This book is not a study book, but a book designed to use English in a meaningful way.

I will tell you how to use the book in a simple but clear way.

1. Do not think that you study English. Instead, read the book.

2. **Read the book from level 1.** Even if level 1 looks very easy, you should read level 1 first to move up to the next level with ease. It's just like climbing the stairs. When you go upstairs, you place your foot on the first stair and then go up to the next one.

3. **If you see a word you don't know, don't consult a Dictionary.** Again, this is a book. The book must be read. It's just like we don't consult an English dictionary when we usually read an English book.

4. **If you have read all the way to level 5, now read books backwards in order of level 4 and 3.** You will learn how to concisely summarize complex sentences.

If you have learned above 4 methods, it is sufficient.

So, let's get started, shall we?

목 차
Contents

단계별 영어 도서
오디오북 채널

머리말 Prologue
독자후기 Reviews
도서 사용법 Manual

Sleeping Beauty **LEVEL 1**   7

Chapter 1	The Little Princess and the Six Fairies	8
Chapter 2	The Seventh Fairy	13
Chapter 3	The Gifts from the Fairies	18
Chapter 4	The Sleeping Princess	24
Chapter 5	One Hundred Years Later	34
Chapter 6	The Princess Wakes Up	37

Sleeping Beauty **LEVEL 2**   49

Chapter 1	The Little Princess and the Six Fairies	50
Chapter 2	The Seventh Fairy	55
Chapter 3	The Gifts from the Fairies	60
Chapter 4	The Sleeping Princess	66
Chapter 5	One Hundred Years Later	76
Chapter 6	The Princess Wakes Up	79

Sleeping Beauty **LEVEL 3**   **89**

Chapter 1	The Little Princess and the Six Fairies	**90**
Chapter 2	The Seventh Fairy	**92**
Chapter 3	The Gifts from the Fairies	**96**
Chapter 4	The Sleeping Princess	**102**
Chapter 5	One Hundred Years Later	**108**
Chapter 6	The Princess Wakes Up	**111**

Sleeping Beauty **LEVEL 4**   **117**

Chapter 1	The Little Princess and the Six Fairies	**118**
Chapter 2	The Seventh Fairy	**120**
Chapter 3	The Gifts from the Fairies	**124**
Chapter 4	The Sleeping Princess	**129**
Chapter 5	One Hundred Years Later	**135**
Chapter 6	The Princess Wakes Up	**138**

Sleeping Beauty **LEVEL 5**   **145**

Chapter 1	The Little Princess and the Six Fairies	**146**
Chapter 2	The Seventh Fairy	**148**
Chapter 3	The Gifts from the Fairies	**152**
Chapter 4	The Sleeping Princess	**157**
Chapter 5	One Hundred Years Later	**162**
Chapter 6	The Princess Wakes Up	**165**

5 STEP ENGLISH
Sleeping Beauty

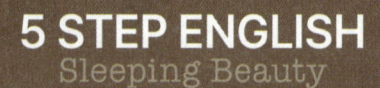

LEVEL 1

단어(Words)

610개

LOW　　　　　　MIDDLE　　　　　　HIGH

문장수(Sentences)

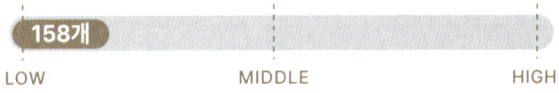

158개

LOW　　　　　　MIDDLE　　　　　　HIGH

문장길이(Sentence Length)

3.9

LOW　　　　　　MIDDLE　　　　　　HIGH

읽는 시간(Reading time)

2분 26초

LOW　　　　　　MIDDLE　　　　　　HIGH

말하는 시간(Speaking Time)

4분 41초

LOW　　　　　　MIDDLE　　　　　　HIGH

LEVEL 1

Chapter 1

The Little Princess and the Six Fairies

A King and a Queen lived together.

The King and Queen had no child.

But then they had a baby girl.
The kingdom was happy.

The King and Queen had a party.
They asked six fairies to come.

Chapter 2

The Seventh Fairy

The six fairies came to the party.

The King and Queen welcomed the fairies.

There was a lot of food at the party.

The dishes were gold.
The fairies had pretty cups.

Everything was beautiful.
The fairies were happy.

There was a big sound.
The bad fairy came.
The bad fairy walked into
the party.

"You asked my sisters to
come. You did not ask me,"
the bad fairy said.

The Queen was scared.
But the Queen welcomed
the bad fairy.
But there was no cup for
the bad fairy.
The bad fairy was angry.

Chapter 3

The Gifts from the Fairies

After the party, the Princess came in.
The Princess smiled.

The first fairy said, "My gift to the Princess is happiness."

"My gift is money," said the second fairy.

"My gift is health," said the third fairy.

"My gift is beauty," said the fourth fairy.

"My gift is fun," said the fifth fairy.

The sixth fairy was thinking. But the bad fairy came.

"She will hurt her finger on a pin. She will die," the bad fairy said.

But the sixth fairy said, "The Princess will not die. She will sleep. A Prince will kiss the Princess. She will wake up."

The bad fairy was angry. She left the party.

The other fairies went home.
They were sad.

The King threw away all the pins.
The pins were gone.
The King was happy again.

The King and Queen were happy.

The Princess grew up.
The Princess was beautiful.

Chapter 4

The Sleeping Princess

One day, the King and Queen went on a trip.

The Princess went to a high tower.

The Princess saw the stairs.
She went up.
She went to the top.
She saw a door.

The Princess opened the door.
The Princess saw an old woman.
The old woman had something new.

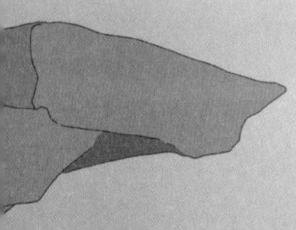

The Princess had never seen this new thing before. The Princess went into the room.

"What are you doing?" the Princess asked.
"I am working," said the old woman.

"What is that?"
"That is a pin."

The Princess touched the pin.
The pin hurt her finger.
The Princess slept.

The King and Queen came home.
They fell asleep. Everyone in the castle slept.

Then a forest grew around
the castle.
The forest was very big.

The Princess slept.
But people did not forget
the Princess.

After many years, everyone forgot about the Princess.

Chapter 5

One Hundred Years Later

After many years, a Prince came by the castle.
The Prince saw a small house.
There was a man in the house.
He was very old.

"What is that?" the Prince asked.

"It is a forest. There is a castle in the forest. A Princess is sleeping in the castle."

"A Princess is sleeping there? Has she slept for a long time?" asked the Prince.

"A long time," said the old man.

Chapter 6

The Princess Wakes Up

The Prince went close to the forest.
The forest opened up.

The Prince went into the castle.
The Prince was surprised.
Everyone was sleeping.

The Prince went into the tower.

A woman was there.
The Prince kissed her.

Then, everyone in the castle woke up.

The Princess opened her eyes.
"Will you marry me?" the Prince asked.
The Princess said, "Yes."

The Prince and Princess got married.

The Prince and Princess lived happily ever after.

5 STEP ENGLISH
Sleeping Beauty

LEVEL 2

단어(Words)

876개

LOW　　　　　　MIDDLE　　　　　　HIGH

문장수(Sentences)

140개

LOW　　　　　　MIDDLE　　　　　　HIGH

문장길이(Sentence Length)

6.3

LOW　　　　　　MIDDLE　　　　　　HIGH

읽는 시간(Reading time)

3분 30초

LOW　　　　　　MIDDLE　　　　　　HIGH

말하는 시간(Speaking Time)

6분 44초

LOW　　　　　　MIDDLE　　　　　　HIGH

LEVEL 2

Chapter 1

The Little Princess and the Six Fairies

A King and a Queen lived together. They did not have a child.

But one day, they had a little daughter. The kingdom was happy.

The King and Queen had a party. They asked six special fairies to come.

But the Queen forgot to ask a seventh fairy. This fairy was very bad.

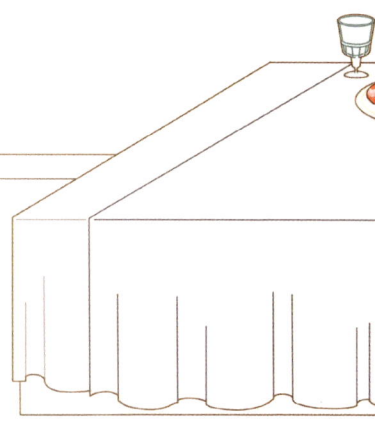

Chapter 2

The Seventh Fairy

The six good fairies came to the party.

The King and Queen welcomed them.

The fairies went into the hall. There was delicious food there.

The dishes were gold, and the fairies had pretty cups.

They had the most beautiful cups in the world.

Everything was beautiful and the fairies were happy.

There was a loud sound outside. The bad fairy came.

The Queen looked outside. The Queen was scared.

The bad fairy had dragons. The bad fairy walked into the party.

The bad fairy cried. "You asked my sisters to come, but you did not ask me."

The Queen did not know what to say. The Queen was scared. But the Queen welcomed the bad fairy.

The bad fairy sat next to the King. But there was no pretty cup for her. When the bad fairy saw the other cups, she was angry.

Chapter 3

The Gifts from the Fairies

After the party, the little Princess came into the room. The little Princess smiled.

The little Princess looked so lovely. Everyone loved the little Princess.

The first fairy said, "My gift to the Princess is happiness."

"I will give her money," said the second fairy.
"She will be healthy," said the third fairy.
"And I will give her beauty," said the fourth fairy.
"And fun. That is my gift to her," said the fifth fairy.

When the sixth fairy was thinking, the bad fairy came out.

"When she is seventeen, she will prick her finger on a pin. She will die," the bad fairy said.

The Queen cried, and the King was scared.

But the sixth fairy said, "The Princess will not die. She will sleep for a long time. Everyone will sleep with her. A Prince will kiss the Princess and she will wake up."

The bad fairy was angry. She ran outside. She left the party.

The other fairies also left the party. They were sad.

The King sent a message. The King threw away all the pins.

There were no more pins. There were no more sharp things. He was happy again.

The King and the Queen were happy.

Everything was fine for a long time. The Princess grew up. She was beautiful.

Chapter 4

The Sleeping Princess

One day, the King and Queen went on a trip.

The Princess went up to a high tower. The Princess wanted to see her parents.

The Princess saw the stairs. She went up and up. Then she was at the top of the tower. She saw a door with a key.

The Princess opened the door. The Princess saw a room. There was an old woman in the room. The old woman had a wheel.

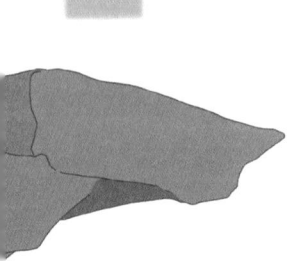

The Princess had naver seen it before. The Princess went into the room. The Princess came close to the old woman.

"What are you doing?" the Princess asked.

"I am working," said the old woman.
"What is that?"
"That is a pin."
"I like it," said the Princess.

The Princess touched the pin. The pin pricked her finger. She went to sleep.

Now it was quiet in the castle. The King and Queen came home.

When they went inside, they went to sleep. The animals slept. The people in the castle slept. Everyone and everything slept.

Then a forest grew around the castle. The forest grew very big and tall.

The Princess slept. But people did not forget the Princess. Many people came to the forest. But they could not go inside.

After many years, everyone forgot about the Princess.

Chapter 5

One Hundred Years Later

After many years, a Prince came by the castle. The Prince was hunting. He was hot and thirsty. The prince saw a small house. He stopped to get some water.

The man in the house was very old. The Prince looked around.

"It is very dark over there. What is over there?" he asked. "It is a forest. There is a castle in the forest. A Princess is sleeping in the castle. My grandfather told me this," the old man said.

"A Princess has been sleeping there? For how long?" asked the Prince.

"I don't know. A long time," said the old man.

The Prince thanked the old man. Then the Prince went to the forest.

Chapter 6

The Princess Wakes Up

The Prince came to the forest.
The flowers grew in the forest.
The forest opened up for the Prince.

The Prince went to the castle. The Prince looked around. The Prince was surprised. The animals were sleeping. The people were sleeping too.

The Prince went into the castle. The Prince looked around the rooms. Then the Prince came to the tower.

There was a young woman inside. The Prince kissed her.

Then, everyone in the castle woke up. The King and Queen woke up. The people woke up. The animals woke up.

The Princess opened her eyes. The Princess loved the Prince.

"Will you marry me?" he asked. The Princess said, "Yes."

The Prince and Princess got married.

The six fairies came to the wedding.

LEVEL 3

단어(Words)

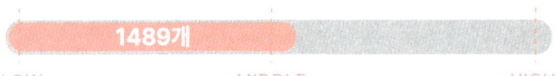

1489개

LOW　　　　　　MIDDLE　　　　　　HIGH

문장수(Sentences)

181개

LOW　　　　　　MIDDLE　　　　　　HIGH

문장길이(Sentence Length)

8.2

LOW　　　　　　MIDDLE　　　　　　HIGH

읽는 시간(Reading time)

5분 57초

LOW　　　　　　MIDDLE　　　　　　HIGH

말하는 시간(Speaking Time)

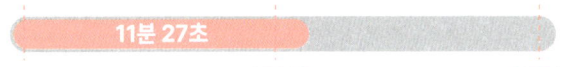

11분 27초

LOW　　　　　　MIDDLE　　　　　　HIGH

LEVEL 3

Chapter 1

The Little Princess and the Six Fairies

There was a King and a Queen who were married. They had no children. But one day, they had a little daughter. There was a celebration in the kingdom.

It was time for a ceremony in the church. The King and Queen held a feast.

They asked six fairies to be the Princess's godmothers. But the Queen forgot to invite a seventh fairy. This fairy was powerful and also very bad.

Chapter 2

The Seventh Fairy

It was the day of the church ceremony. The six good fairies came in carriages. They were welcomed by the King and Queen. After talking to them, the King and Queen showed the fairies the way to the hall. Everything there was wonderful. There were delicious fruits and meats there, along with bread.

The dishes were gold, and each fairy was given a wine glass. One glass was made of diamond. One glass was made of ruby, and one glass was made of emerald. Even in their fairy houses, they didn't have such lovely wine glasses. The fairies were excited about everything.

They were all sitting down. There was a loud noise outside. The Queen looked outside and she was shocked.

The bad fairy came. The Queen thought the bad fairy came to do something evil. Her carriage was black, and she had four dragons. The bad fairy came out of her carriage and walked into the hall with her staff.

"How did this happen?" she cried to the Queen. "All my sisters were asked to come, but I was not asked."

The Queen did not know how to answer this. The Queen was nervous. But the Queen made the seventh fairy feel welcome.

The seventh fairy sat next to the King. The King and Queen said they knew the fairy would come. But there was no wine glass for the seventh fairy. When she saw the other wine glasses, she became angry. Her eyes were red. The seventh fairy ate and drank, but she did not say anything.

Chapter 3

The Gifts from the Fairies

After the feast, they brought the little Princess into the room. She smiled so nicely and looked so pure. Only a person with a bad heart could plan something bad for her.

The first fairy held the child and said, "My gift to the Princess shall be happiness."

"Gold is good," said the second fairy, "so I will give her the gift of wealth."

"She shall be healthy," said the third.

"And I," said the fourth, "I will give her the gift of beauty."

"And fun," said the fifth. "That is my gift to her."

The sixth fairy was still thinking. Then the bad fairy came out. While the other fairies were talking, the bad fairy was very angry.

"And I say," she said, "that when she's seventeen, she shall prick her finger on a pin and die."

The Queen cried, and the King's face was white. But the sixth fairy said something.

"Wait," she said. "I didn't say anything yet. I say that the Princess will not die. She will sleep for one hundred years, and everyone will sleep with her. After that, a Prince will kiss her and she will wake up."

When the evil fairy heard this, she was very angry. But the sixth fairy had already spoken. There was nothing the evil fairy could do. She ran out of the castle and jumped into her carriage, and went far away.

The other fairies also went away. They were sad. They knew that later, something bad was going to happen to the Princess.

The King told everyone to take away every pin from the land. He felt very happy again. If all the pins were gone, the Princess could not prick her finger. If she did not prick her finger, she would not sleep.

So the King and Queen were glad. Everything was fine in the castle for seventeen years. Everything that the fairies said came true. The Princess was beautiful. She was funny and kind. She had health, wealth, and happiness. She smiled and was happy.

Chapter 4

The Sleeping Princess

One day the King and Queen were out traveling. The Princess climbed up into a high tower. This was her first time going into the tower. She wanted to see her parents come back home.

She found the stairs. She climbed up until she was high above the castle.

After a while, she came to the top of the tower. She found an iron door with an old key inside.

The Princess turned the key. The door opened. The Princess saw a room. Inside the room was an old woman. The old woman was sitting at a spinning wheel.

The Princess had never seen a spinning wheel before. It was so new to her. The Princess walked into the room and came close to the old woman. The Princess wanted to see it better.

"What are you doing?" the Princess asked.

"I am making cloth," answered the old woman.

"And what is that little thing moving so fast?"

"That is a pin."

"It is very nice," said the Princess, and she lifted up her hand to touch it.

The pin pricked her finger. The Princess fell onto a sofa and went to sleep.

Everyone in the castle fell asleep quickly. The King and Queen came home from their trip. They went into the castle. Then they fell asleep. The King's helpers also fell asleep. The animals in the garden slept, and the birds slept too. The boy in the kitchen slept. The cook was not angry at the boy because she was asleep too. The food was not burned, because the fire was also sleeping. Even the bugs in the flowers were not moving. Everyone and everything slept.

Then a magic forest grew very fast all around the castle. The forest was like a wall. The forest grew very thick and tall. Nothing could be seen.

The Princess slept, but people did not forget about her. Many princes and heroes came and tried to cut down the trees to save the Princess. But the tree branches were hard, and they grew back very quickly.

After many years, the heroes who tried to save the Princess got married and had children. The heroes' children also grew up and got married. In the end, everyone forgot about the Princess.

Chapter 5

One Hundred Years Later

After one hundred years, a Prince came by the castle. The Prince was young and handsome. He had been hunting. He was riding his horse very fast. He left the other people behind. The Prince was hot and tired. He saw a small shack. He stopped there to get some water.

The man who lived in the shack was very old. He gave some water to the Prince. After the Prince had a drink of water, he sat for a while and looked around.

"I see a large dark shadow over there. It looks like a cloud. What is in the darkness?" he asked.

"I don't know," said the old man.

"I never went there. But my grandfather told me that it was a magic forest. He said there was a castle in the middle of the forest. He said that a Princess was asleep inside it."

"And how long has she been sleeping there?" asked the Prince.

"I don't know. She has been there for a long, long time," answered the old man.

The Prince thanked the old man for telling him the story. Then the Prince rode into the magic forest. He went very fast.

Chapter 6

The Princess Wakes Up

The forest was dark like a cloud. But when the Prince came close to the forest, the flowers started to grow. When the Prince walked into the forest, the tree branches opened up.

The Prince rode down the road, and then he came to the castle. He entered the garden and looked around. He was amazed. The dogs were sleeping. The horses were sleeping. The doormen were sleeping.

The Prince went into the castle. He looked around the rooms. No one woke up to stop the Prince.

After a while, the Prince found the stairs and he climbed them. He came to the tower room, and then he stopped.

There was a young woman on a sofa. The Prince looked at her and kissed her.

At that moment, the castle was full of sounds. Everyone was waking up. The King and Queen woke up and stretched. The doormen woke up from sleep. The horses ran around. The dogs barked. The food in the kitchen was burning. The cook was angry. The King's helpers smiled.

In the tower, the Princess opened her eyes. When she saw the Prince, she fell in love with him. The Prince took her hand.

"Will you be my wife?" he asked. The Princess answered, "Yes."

The Prince and Princess got married. The six fairies came to the wedding with beautiful gifts.

The seventh fairy died because she was so angry. But the Prince and Princess lived happily ever after.

5 STEP ENGLISH
Sleeping Beauty

LEVEL 4

단어(Words)

1922개

LOW　　　　　　MIDDLE　　　　　　HIGH

문장수(Sentences)

169개

LOW　　　　　　MIDDLE　　　　　　HIGH

문장길이(Sentence Length)

11.4

LOW　　　　　　MIDDLE　　　　　　HIGH

읽는 시간(Reading time)

7분 41초

LOW　　　　　　MIDDLE　　　　　　HIGH

말하는 시간(Speaking Time)

14분 47초

LOW　　　　　　MIDDLE　　　　　　HIGH

Chapter 1

The Little Princess and the Six Fairies

There was a King and a Queen who had been married for a long time. But they had no children. However, one day they finally had a little daughter. This was an important day of celebration in the kingdom.

When the time came for the Princess's baptism, a feast was prepared. The King and Queen asked six fairies to be the Princess's godmothers. The

Queen forgot to invite a seventh fairy. It was too bad, because this fairy was the most powerful of them all. She was also very evil and hateful.

Chapter 2

The Seventh Fairy

On the day of the Princess's baptism, the six good fairies came in chariots pulled by birds.

They were welcomed by the King and Queen, and after talking, the King and Queen led them to the hall. A feast was prepared. Everything there was very impressive. There were delicious fruits, meats, bread, and many wonderful things.

The dishes were made of gold, and

each fairy received a goblet. Each goblet was made from a single stone. One goblet was made of diamond, one of sapphire, one of ruby, one of emerald, one of amethyst, and one of topaz. The fairies were very pleased with the beauty of everything. Even in their fairy palaces, they didn't have such lovely goblets.

They were about to take their places, but there was a loud noise outside. The Queen looked out of the window and almost fainted. The bad fairy had arrived. The bad fairy was not invited to the feast. The Queen feared that this fairy came to do something terrible. Her chariot was black, and four dragons pulled it with fiery eyes and golden bodies. The fairy quickly got out of her chariot and walked into the hall with her staff in her hand.

"How can it be? How can it be?" she cried to the Queen.
"Here, all my sisters have been invited to come, and only I have been forgotten."

The Queen did not know how to answer her. The Queen was fearful. However, the Queen didn't show her fear and she made the seventh fairy feel welcome like the other fairies. The seventh fairy sat on the right side of the King, and the

King and Queen acted like they expected her to come.

However, there was no special goblet for her. When she saw the other goblets that were given to the six fairies, her face was full of envy. She had fire in her eyes. She ate and drank, but she never spoke.

Chapter 3

The Gifts from the Fairies

After the feast, the little Princess was brought into the room. She smiled so sweetly and looked so pure that only a bad heart could have planned something terrible for her.

The first fairy took the child in her arms and said, "My gift to the Princess shall be happiness, because happiness is better than gold."

"Gold is good," said the second fairy, "so I will give her the gift of wealth."

"She shall be healthy," said the third,

"because wealth is nothing without health."

"And I," said the fourth, "will give her the gift of beauty to touch everyone's hearts."

"And humor to tickle everyone's ears," said the fifth. "That is my gift to her."

The sixth fairy hesitated. At that moment, the evil one came forward. While the others were talking, she was getting very angry.

"And I say," she cried, "that when she turns

seventeen, she shall prick her finger on a spindle and die."

When the Queen heard this, she cried out loud, and the King's face turned pale. But the sixth fairy came forward.

"Wait a moment," she said. "I have not spoken yet. I cannot cancel what our sister did, but I say that the Princess will not really die. She will fall into a deep sleep for one hundred years, and everyone shall sleep with her. At that time, she will receive a special kiss, and she will wake up."

When the wicked fairy heard this, she was furious, but the sixth fairy had already spoken. The wicked fairy couldn't do anything else. She ran out of the castle and jumped into her chariot. The dragons took her somewhere far away. Nobody knows where she went.

The other fairies also went away, and they were sad because they knew what would happen to the Princess.

The King commanded that every spinning wheel and spindle be removed from the land. When this was done, the King felt very happy again. If all the spindles were gone, the Princess could not prick her finger. If she did not prick her finger, she would not fall into a magical sleep.

So the King and Queen were satisfied, and everything was fine in the castle for seventeen years. Everything that the fairies promised came true. The Princess was so beautiful that everyone who saw her was surprised. She was so funny and kind that everyone loved her. She had health, wealth, happiness, and she smiled and was happy all the time.

Chapter 4

The Sleeping Princess

One day the King and Queen went on a journey. The Princess decided to climb up into a high tower. She had never been there before. She waited to see her parents come back home.

She found the stairs that led to the tower, and she climbed them. She climbed them up and up and up, until she was high above the castle rooftops. Finally, she came to the very top of the tower, and she found an iron door with an old key in it.

The Princess turned the key, and the door opened. Behind the door, she saw a room. Inside the room, an old woman sat at a spinning wheel.

The Princess had never seen a spinning wheel before. It was very interesting to her. She entered the room and came close to the old woman. She wanted to see it better.

"What are you doing?" she asked.

"I am spinning," answered the old woman.

"And what is that little thing that moves around so fast?"

"That is a spindle."

"It is very interesting," said the Princess, and she stretched out her hand to touch it. Then the spindle pricked her finger. The Princess sighed, her eyes closed, and she fell back onto a sofa and into a deep sleep.

A silence also quickly came down on everyone in the castle. The King and Queen had just come home from their journey.

They came down from their horses, entered the castle, and just then, they fell asleep. The advisors who followed them into the castle also fell asleep. The dogs and horses in the garden slept, and the birds on the roof slept too. The boy who took care of the fire in the kitchen slept. The cook was not mad at the boy because she was asleep too. The food was not burned by the fire, because the fire was also sleeping. Even the bugs in the castle and the bees among the flowers stopped moving. Everyone and everything slept.

Then a magic forest quickly grew all around the castle and encircled it like a wall. The forest grew so thick and tall that not even a tower in the castle could be seen.

Even though the Princess slept, she was not forgotten. Many brave princes and heroes came and tried to cut through the forest to save her. But the tree branches were as hard as iron, and they grew back as fast as they were cut down. The branches were so twisted that no one could get through them.

Years passed by. The brave heroes who had tried to save the Princess grew old and had children. Their children also grew up and got married. At last, everyone forgot about the Princess, or she was remembered only as an old story.

Chapter 5

One Hundred Years Later

After a hundred years, a young and handsome Prince came by the castle. He had been hunting, and he had ridden so fast that he had left his hunting helpers behind. Now he was hot and tired, and seeing a hut, he stopped to ask for a drink of water.

The man who lived in the hut was very old. He brought the water the Prince asked for. After the Prince had a drink of water, he sat for a while and looked around.

"What is that darkness, like a cloud, that I see over there?" he asked.

"I cannot tell you exactly," said the old man, "because it is far away and I have never been there. My grandfather once told me that it was a magic forest. He said there was a secret castle deep in the middle of it and that a Princess was asleep inside it."

"And how long has she been asleep?" asked the Prince. His heart was beating very fast.

"I cannot say," answered the old man, "but a long, long time. My grandfather was an old man when he told me. He could not even remember her."

The Prince thanked the old man for what he had told him. Then he rode away toward the magic forest. He went very quickly.

Chapter 6

The Princess Wakes Up

When the Prince was far from the forest, the forest looked like a dark cloud. But when he got closer, the flowers began to grow. The tree branches began to grow as well. When the Prince came closer to the branches, the flowers were budding everywhere. When the Prince came to the front of the forest, the branches opened up and there was a road in front of him.

Along this road the Prince rode, and soon he came to the palace. He entered the garden and looked around. He was amazed. The dogs were sleeping on the ground and they never woke up when the Prince came close. The horses stood like statues. The gatekeepers slept leaning on their weapons.

The Prince stepped down from his horse and went into the palace. He looked in one room after another, and no one woke up to stop him.

Finally, he came to the stairs that led to the tower. He climbed them, up and up, just like the Princess had done many years before him.

He came to the tower room, and then he stopped and stood amazed. There was a young woman on a couch. She was more beautiful than the Prince had ever imagined. He could hardly believe there was such beauty in the world. He looked and looked and then he bent over and kissed her.

At that moment, sounds of everyone waking up filled the castle. The King and Queen, in their room, stretched and rubbed their eyes. The gatekeepers woke up from sleep. The horses stamped, and the dogs jumped up barking. The meat in the kitchen was burning, and the cook was mad at the boy. The advisors smiled and bowed.

Up in the tower, the Princess opened her eyes. After she saw the Prince, she loved him. The Prince took her hand and lifted her from the couch.

"Will you be my beloved wife?" he asked. And the Princess answered yes.

And so the Prince and Princess were married. There was a grand celebration. The six fairies came to the wedding and brought gifts. The gifts were the most beautiful gifts in the world. The seventh fairy was extremely angry. She was so angry that she could not live any longer, and then, she died. But the Prince and Princess lived happily ever after.

5 STEP ENGLISH
Sleeping Beauty

LEVEL 5

단어(Words)

1984개

LOW　　　　　　　　MIDDLE　　　　　　　　HIGH

문장수(Sentences)

123개

LOW　　　　　　　　MIDDLE　　　　　　　　HIGH

문장길이(Sentence Length)

16.1

LOW　　　　　　　　MIDDLE　　　　　　　　HIGH

읽는 시간(Reading time)

7분 56초

LOW　　　　　　　　MIDDLE　　　　　　　　HIGH

말하는 시간(Speaking Time)

15분 15초

LOW　　　　　　　　MIDDLE　　　　　　　　HIGH

THE ORIGINAL TEXT

Chapter 1

The Little Princess and the Six Fairies

Once, there was a King and Queen who had no children, although they had been married for many years. At last, however, they gave birth to a little daughter. This event was worthy of celebration throughout the kingdom.

When the time came for the little Princess to be christened, a grand feast was prepared, and six powerful fairies were asked to be her godmothers. Unfortunately, the Queen forgot to invite the seventh fairy, the most powerful of them all, who was also very wicked and malicious.

Chapter 2

The Seventh Fairy

On the Princess's christening day, the six good fairies came early in chariots drawn by butterflies, doves, wrens, and other birds. They were welcomed by the King and Queen, and after talking, the King and Queen led them to the hall where the feast had been set out. Everything there was very magnificent. There were delicious fruits and meats and pastries and everything that could be thought of.

The dishes were made of gold, and each fairy received a goblet cut from a single precious stone. One was made of diamond, one of sapphire, one of ruby, one of emerald, one of amethyst, and one of topaz. The fairies were delighted with the beauty of everything. Even in their own fairy palaces, they didn't have goblets as lovely as those the King had made for them.

They were just about to take their places at the table when a loud noise was heard outside on the terrace. The Queen looked out of the window and almost fainted at what she saw. The bad fairy had arrived. She had come uninvited, and the Queen feared that she came to do something terrible. Her chariot was made of black iron and was drawn by four dragons with flaming eyes and brass scales. The fairy quickly sprang from her chariot and walked into the hall with her staff in her hand.

"How is this? How is this?" she cried to the Queen. "Here, all my sisters have been invited to come and bring their gifts to the Princess, and only I have been forgotten."

The Queen did not know how to answer. She was frightened. However, she tried to hide her fear and made the seventh fairy as welcome as the others. A place was set for her at the King's right hand, and he and the Queen tried to pretend they had expected her to come. However, there was no precious goblet for her, and when she saw the ones that had been given to the six other fairies, her face grew green with envy, and her eyes flashed fire. She ate and drank, but she never said a word.

Chapter 3

The Gifts from the Fairies

After the feast, the little Princess was brought into the room, and she smiled so sweetly and looked so innocent that only a wicked heart could have planned something awful for her.

The first fairy took the child in her arms and said, "My gift to the Princess shall be that of contentment, for contentment is better than gold."

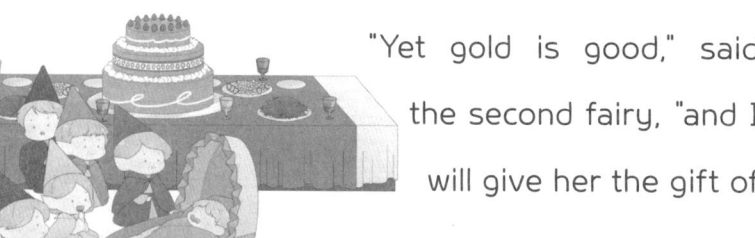

"Yet gold is good," said the second fairy, "and I will give her the gift of wealth."

"She shall be healthy," said the third, "because wealth is of little use without it."

"And I," said the fourth, "will give her the gift of beauty to win everyone's hearts."

"And wit to charm everyone's ears," said the fifth. "That is my gift to her."

The sixth fairy hesitated, and in that moment, the wicked one stepped forward. While the others had spoken, she had been swelling with anger.

"And I say," cried she, "that in her seventeenth year, she shall prick her finger on a spindle and die."

When the Queen heard this, she shrieked

aloud, and the King grew as pale as death. But the sixth fairy stepped forward.

"Wait," she said. "I have not spoken yet. I cannot undo what our sister has done, but I say that the Princess shall not really die. She shall fall into a deep sleep that will last a hundred years, and everyone in the castle shall sleep with her. At the end of that time, she will arise when she receives a special kiss."

When the wicked fairy heard this, she was filled with rage, but the sixth fairy had already spoken; the wicked fairy couldn't do anything else. She rushed out of the castle and jumped into her chariot, and the dragons carried her away, and where she went, no one knew or cared.

The other fairies also went away, and they were sad because of what was going to happen to the Princess.

The King immediately gave orders that every spinning wheel and spindle in the land should be destroyed, and when this was done, he felt very happy again. For if all the spindles were gone, the Princess could not prick her finger on one; and if she did not prick her finger, she would not fall into the enchanted sleep.

So the King and Queen were content, and everything was fine in the castle for seventeen years. Everything that the fairies had promised to give the Princess came true. She was so beautiful that everyone who saw her was in awe, and she was so witty and kind that everyone loved her. Besides this, she had health, wealth, and contentment, and she smiled and was happy from morning until night.

Chapter 4

The Sleeping Princess

One day the King and Queen went away on a journey, and the Princess decided to climb up a high tower where she had never been before and watch for her parents to return.

She found the stairs that led to the tower, and she climbed them, up and up and up, until she was high above the roofs of the castle. At last, she reached the very top of the tower, and she found an iron door with

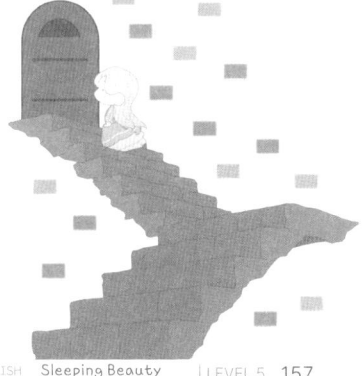

a rusty key in it.

The Princess turned the key, and the door swung open. Beyond the door, she saw a room, and an old woman with many wrinkles sat at a spinning wheel.

The Princess had never seen a spinning wheel before. It was very interesting to her. She entered the room and stood close to the old woman so she could see it better.

"What are you doing?" she asked.

"I am spinning," answered the old woman.

"And what is that little thing that flies around so fast?"

"That is a spindle."

"It is very interesting," said the Princess, and she reached out her hand to touch it. Then the point of the spindle pricked her finger, and at once the Princess sighed, and her eyes closed, and she fell back onto a couch in a deep sleep.

Immediately a silence also fell upon everyone in the castle. The King and Queen had just returned from their journey; they had come down from their horses and had entered the castle, and just then, they fell asleep. The courtiers who followed them also fell asleep. The dogs and horses in the courtyard slept, and the pigeons on the eaves slept too. The boy who turned the spit in the kitchen slept, and the cook did not scold him, for she was asleep too. The meat did not burn because the fire was also sleeping. Even the flies in the castle and the bees among the flowers hung motionless. Everyone and everything slept.

Then an enchanted forest quickly grew all around the castle and surrounded it like a wall. The forest grew so thick and tall that finally not even the tallest tower of the castle could be seen.

Even though the Princess slept, she was not forgotten. Many brave princes and heroes came and tried to cut their way through the forest to rescue her, but the boughs and branches were as hard as iron, and they grew back as fast as they were cut;

also they were twisted so closely together that no one could squeeze between them. As years passed by, the brave heroes who had tried to rescue the Princess grew old and had children of their own. Their children, too, grew up and married, and at last everyone forgot about the Princess, or she was remembered only as an old tale.

Chapter 5

One Hundred Years Later

A hundred years passed, and then a young and handsome Prince came by the castle. He had been hunting, and he had ridden so fast and eagerly that he had left his huntsmen far behind. Now he was hot and tired, and seeing a hut, he stopped and asked for a drink of water.

The man who lived in the hut was very old. He brought the water the Prince asked for, and after the Prince had a drink, he sat for a while and looked around.

"What is that darkness, like a cloud, that I see over there?" he asked.

"I cannot tell you for sure," said the old man, "for it is far away, and I have never gone to see it, but my grandfather once told me that it was an enchanted forest. He said there was a castle hidden deep in the middle of it and that a Princess was asleep inside it."

"And how long has she been sleeping?" asked the Prince, and his heart started to beat very rapidly.

"That I cannot say," answered the old man, "but a long, long time. My grandfather was an old man when he told me, and he could not remember her."

The Prince thanked the old man for what he had told him, and then he rode away toward the enchanted forest, and he could not go fast enough.

Chapter 6

The Princess Wakes Up

When he was far away from the forest, it looked like a dark cloud, but it began to grow rosy as he got closer. All the boughs and briers had begun to bud. By the time he was close to them, they were in full flower, and when he reached the edge of the forest, the branches divided, leaving an open path before him.

Along this path the Prince rode, and before long, he came to the palace. He entered the courtyard and looked around in wonder. The dogs lay sleeping in the sunshine and never woke up when he came near. The horses stood like statues. The guards slept, leaning on their arms.

The Prince dismounted and went into the palace; he went through one room after another, and no one woke up to stop him. At last he came to the stairway that led to the tower and he climbed it,—up and up, as the Princess had done before him. He reached the tower-room, and then he stopped and stood amazed. There on the couch was a young woman more beautiful than he had ever dreamed of. He could scarcely believe that there was such beauty in the world. He looked and looked and then he bent over and kissed her.

At once at that exact moment—the sounds of everyone waking up filled the castle. The King and Queen, down in the throne room, stirred and rubbed their eyes. The guards started from their sleep. The horsesstamped, the dogs sprang up barking. The meat in the kitchen began to burn, and the cook

scolded the boy. The courtiers smiled and bowed.

Up in the tower, the Princess opened her eyes, and as soon as she saw the Prince, she loved him. He took her hand and raised her from the couch.

"Will you be my own dear bride?" he said. And the Princess answered yes.

And so they were married with a grand celebration, and the six fairies came to the wedding and brought gifts more beautiful than were ever seen before. As for the seventh fairy, she was extremely angry. She burst with anger, and then, she died. But the Prince and Princess lived happily ever after.